D0473745

The Nosher's Essential Israeli Dishes

DESIGNED BY **GRACE YAGEL**

Cover image by Rachel Simons

The Nosher's Essential Israeli Dishes

A Recipe Collection

Israeli food is one of the most dynamic and popular cuisines worldwide today, yet it's hard to define it precisely because it encompasses such a variety of dishes from around the world. The diversity of influences and vibrancy of colors, spices like za'atar and cardamom, and varied cooking methods all make for foods that are as exciting to eat as they are to look at and learn about. Homegrown Israeli dishes, like ptitim, krembo and stuffed pita sandwiches are also essential to understanding how Israelis eat today and the evolution of the cuisine. In this recipe collection we have brought together tried-and-true Israeli classics like schnitzel, pashtida and shakshuka, dishes that Israelis eat every day at home with short stories that explain their place at the table.

This is merely a taste, and our wish is that you continue to visit The Nosher for more recipes. In the meantime, we hope the pages of the collection get covered with a little bit of splattered oil, a lot of spice and enjoyed over and over again.

A very special thanks to our talented contributors Sonya Sanford, Vered Guttman, Chaya Rapaport, Emanuelle Lee, Lior Mashiach, Micah Siva, Shlomo Schwartz, Rachel Simons, Mike Solomonov, Danielle Oron and Lynda Balslev for sharing their enticing recipes and the stories behind them.

This book was created by The Nosher, edited by Shannon Sarna and Rachel Myerson and designed by Grace Yagel.

– The Nosher Staff

Table of Contents

HUMMUS

Dips, Sauces & Starters

- MATBUCHA
- HUMMUS
- TAHINI SAUCE
- ZHUG
- AMBA

MATBUCHA

Photo: Sonya Sanford

YIELD: 4-6 SERVINGS

MATBUCHA

Sonya Sanford

Matbucha is a North African salad made of tomatoes and peppers, and means "cooked salad" in Arabic. Jewish immigrants from Morocco, Tunisia, Algeria and Libya brought matbucha with them to Israel, where it has become a staple of Israeli cuisine. Matbucha is nearly as popular as hummus, and the two are usually located right by each other at the grocery store.
Matbucha is typically served at the start of a meal with other dips and salads, known collectively as "salatim." Matbucha varies from kitchen to kitchen; some cooks add onions and/or garlic, and some prefer making it with lots of hot peppers. Adding some fresh chili pepper is traditional; in this recipe, it adds a very mild and subtle heat.

__Note:__ Matbucha can be eaten right after it cools, but it tastes even better the next day. It will last up to one week in the fridge.

INGREDIENTS

- 6 large Roma tomatoes
- 3 medium red bell peppers
- 1 jalapeño or Serrano pepper, seeded and diced fine
- ½ medium yellow onion, diced small
- 2-3 cloves garlic, minced
- 1 tsp salt, or to taste
- ¼ cup olive oil
- 1-2 tsp sugar (optional, or to taste)

DIRECTIONS

1. Line a baking sheet with foil. Set the oven to broil (alternatively, you can char the peppers over a gas flame or grill).

2. Place the tomatoes on one half of the baking sheet, and the peppers on the other half. Place the baking sheet on the top rack of the oven and broil the tomatoes and peppers for 10 minutes, or until blackened on top. Using tongs or a fork, remove the tomatoes. Turn the peppers onto their opposite side and continue to broil them until blackened on both sides, another 8-10 minutes. Watch your tomatoes and peppers carefully, as some ovens will broil them more quickly than others.

3. Once the peppers are blackened on both sides, place them in a bowl and cover it tightly with foil or plastic wrap to let the peppers steam. Prep the other ingredients while the tomatoes and peppers cool. Once cool enough to touch, peel the peppers and remove their seeds, and peel the tomatoes. Dice the peppers and tomatoes and reserve.

4. To a medium pot over medium heat, add the olive oil, diced jalapeño, diced onion and minced garlic. Allow the mixture to cook and soften for 4-5 minutes until the onion and garlic are aromatic but before they start turning brown. Add the peeled, diced peppers and tomatoes to the mixture, lower the heat, and let the matbucha simmer for 90 minutes, or until most of the liquid has evaporated and the mixture significantly thickens. Stir every 10-15 minutes. Matbucha can take more or less time depending on the size of the pot you use or the amount of liquid in the tomatoes. If the mixture still has a lot of liquid, continue to cook it for up to 2 hours.

5. Once cooked, allow the matbucha to fully cool and then refrigerate.

HUMMUS

YIELD: 4-6 SERVINGS

HUMMUS

Danielle Oron

Hummus isn't just a snack or a dip for Israelis — it's a full meal. You can serve ground meat, shredded chicken, roasted vegetables or warm chickpeas on top of a plate of perfect hummus for a complete meal. The trick for this creamy hummus made from canned chickpeas is to simmer them with baking soda, which helps break down the skin on each chickpea, ensuring you get that crave-worthy, super smooth hummus. Add your favorite toppings or, as I've done in this recipe, just some extra spices, chopped parsley and a generous drizzle of olive oil.

INGREDIENTS

For the hummus:

- 15.5 oz can chickpeas (make sure to reserve the liquid)
- ½ tsp baking soda
- ½ cup water
- 1 clove garlic

- 1 cup tahini
- 1 Tbsp fresh lemon juice
- a pinch cumin
- 1 tsp kosher salt

To serve:

- extra virgin olive oil
- zhug

- chopped parsley
- za'atar, paprika and/or cumin

DIRECTIONS

1. In a medium pot over medium-high heat, bring the chickpeas, chickpea liquid, baking soda and about ½ cup water to a boil.

2. Immediately turn the heat down to low and skim any foam that rises to the surface. Simmer, stirring occasionally, until the chickpeas are very soft, about 10 minutes.

3. Take off the heat and let it cool for 10 minutes. Drain the chickpeas very well and reserve all the cooking liquid.

4. Place the chickpeas and garlic clove in the bowl of a food processor and blend on high until smooth, scraping down the bowl halfway through, about 2 minutes.

5. Add the tahini, lemon juice, cumin, salt and about ¼ cup of the cooking liquid from the beans, and process until very smooth and light in color, at least 2 minutes. The texture should be like soft-serve ice cream. If it looks too thick, add more cooking liquid (or water). If the hummus is still warm, it will get thicker as it cools, so keep that in mind. Taste and adjust seasoning with salt and lemon juice to your taste.

6. Plate the hummus by swirling it onto a serving dish, making a well in the middle. Drizzle with additional olive oil, garnish with zhug, spices or chopped parsley if desired.

TAHINI SAUCE

TAHINI SAUCE

Shannon Sarna

Basic tahini sauce is made with a mixture of tahini paste, water, lemon juice and garlic. Tahini paste itself is made from toasted ground sesame seeds. Both tahini paste and tahini sauce are staples of Israeli cooking. These days, it's easy to find good-quality tahini paste outside the Middle East; Soom and Seed + Mill are two excellent U.S.-based brands, or look for Har Bracha tahini on Amazon.

INGREDIENTS

- ½ cup good-quality tahini
- ½ cup ice water
- juice ½ a lemon

- ½ tsp salt
- ¼ tsp pepper

DIRECTIONS

1. Place tahini in a small-medium bowl.

2. Add ice water and slowly whisk. Keep adding ice water and whisking until smooth consistency is reached. Don't worry if the tahini seems too thick at first — just keep drizzling in the cold water and it will smooth out.

3. Add the lemon juice, salt and pepper. Adjust seasoning to taste.

ZHUG

Photo: Sonya Sanford

ZHUG

Sonya Sanford

Zhug is a classic Yemenite hot sauce. It is found throughout the Middle East, and was brought to, and made popular in, Israel by Yemenite Jews. It is used to add heat to many dishes, from falafel to shawarma, schnitzel and sabich. There are countless recipes for zhug, but it is always made with a combination of hot green or red peppers and cilantro (AKA coriander). Often, you'll find it includes spices, such as cardamom or caraway.

Note: Zhug will last up to two weeks in the fridge in a well-sealed container, or it can be frozen for up to three months.

INGREDIENTS

- 5-10 small jalapeño peppers (5 for mild, 10 for hot), sliced in half and deseeded
- 1 bunch cilantro
- 1 bunch parsley
- 1 large clove garlic, peeled
- 1 Tbsp ground cardamom

- 2 tsp caraway seeds (optional)
- 1 tsp kosher salt
- juice ½ a lemon
- ¼ cup oil (a mild, neutral oil: sunflower, canola, grapeseed, etc.)

DIRECTIONS

1. To a food processor, add the deseeded jalapeños, parsley, cilantro, garlic, cardamom, caraway and salt. Pulse until finely chopped. If you don't have a food processor, you can also chop the ingredients finely by hand.

2. Transfer the chopped mixture to a bowl. Add the oil and lemon juice, and stir until combined.

AMBA

Photo: Sonya Sanford

YIELD: 3 PINTS

AMBA

Sonya Sanford

Amba is a spiced, pickled mango condiment that made its way to Israel via the Iraqi Jewish community. Traditionally, amba is made by slicing and salting green mangoes, and placing them in a jar in the sun to ferment for five days. Afterward, the mango is removed from the jar and left to dry out in sunlight for 3-4 hours. Once dried, the cured mango is cooked with a variety of spices and aromatics, vinegar is added, and the amba is jarred for use.

This recipe is a quicker, easier way to make the flavorful condiment. You still salt the mango, and you let it sit in that salt overnight, but that's the extent of the wait time. For this recipe any mango will work, but it is best to use ones that are firm and not fully ripe. This recipe makes a mildly spicy amba; you can adjust the level of heat depending on how much chili and cayenne you add. Amba is perfect to serve with shawarma, sabich or fish.

Note: *Amba keeps well in the fridge for two to three weeks.*

INGREDIENTS

- 3 lb or 4 large, firm, unripened mangoes
- 3 Tbsp kosher salt
- 3 Tbsp neutral oil
- 6 cloves garlic, finely minced
- 1 medium Fresno chili, seeded and diced fine, or to taste
- 2 tsp mustard seeds
- 1 Tbsp ground turmeric
- 2 tsp ground fenugreek
- 2 tsp ground coriander
- 2 tsp ground cumin
- pinch of cayenne, or to taste
- 3 Tbsp brown sugar, or to taste (or substitute with your preferred sweetener)
- 1 cup water
- ½ cup white vinegar

DIRECTIONS

1. Peel your mangoes, then slice the fruit around the pit. Dice the mango into small cubes, they do not have to be even or perfect. Add the diced mango to a large non-reactive bowl. Add the salt to the mango and toss until they're well-coated. Cover the bowl and refrigerate for 1 day.

2. After the mango has cured in the fridge, add oil to a large pot or deep sauté pan over medium-low heat. Add the mustard seeds to the oil, and when they begin to make popping sounds add the finely minced garlic and diced chili. Sauté until softened and fragrant but before anything begins to brown, about 2-3 minutes. Add the remaining spices: turmeric, fenugreek, coriander, cumin and cayenne. Stir and sauté for an additional minute.

3. Add the mango, brown sugar and water to the pot. Stir, increase the heat, and bring the liquid up to a simmer. Simmer for 5-6 minutes, or until the mango has softened and the liquid has slightly reduced. Turn off the heat and add the vinegar to the mango mixture. Taste and adjust to your liking by adding more vinegar, sugar, salt or spices, if needed.

4. Using an immersion blender or blender, purée the mango to the desired consistency. I like mine a little chunky with about half of the mango pieces still intact. If you would like your amba smoother you can purée it for longer and add water to thin it out. Note that amba will thicken slightly as it cools.

5. Once cooled, transfer the amba to jars and refrigerate.

SHAWARMA KEBAB

Photo: Chaya Rapaport

Main Dishes

- IRAQI STUFFED TOMATOES AND ONIONS

- SABICH

- SCHNITZEL

- SHAKSHUKA

- PASHTIDA

- CHRAIMEH

- ISRAELI COUSCOUS PILAF

- KTZITZOT PRASA

- CHICKEN SHAWARMA KEBAB

- ROASTED VEGETABLES WITH TAHINI

IRAQI STUFFED TOMATOES AND ONIONS

Photo: Vered Guttman

YIELD: 8 SERVINGS

IRAQI STUFFED TOMATOES AND ONIONS

Vered Guttman

All types of stuffed vegetables are popular throughout the Middle East and Israel. Called memu-laim, a useful catch-all Hebrew term meaning "stuffed," they run the gamut from grape leaves to potatoes to artichoke bottoms. This stuffed onions and tomatoes recipe is an Iraqi-inspired dish that is traditionally served on Shabbat. The onions in this recipe are separated into layers and each layer is stuffed on its own, so a whole onion yields about 6-7 stuffed onions. It's best to use a 12-14 inch round pan with a lid so you can arrange the stuffed onions in one layer, but you can also use a smaller pan and arrange them in two layers.

A note on rice: The rice is soaked in cold water for at least one hour before the rest of the stuffing is added, to make sure it is moist enough and will not dry during the cooking process. When it comes to stuffing the vegetables with the rice mixture, resist the temptation to overstuff. The rice expands as it cooks and will rip the vegetables if they're too full.

INGREDIENTS

- 3 large yellow onions
- 4-6 firm beefsteak tomatoes (or 1 per person)

For the sauce:

- 2⅔ cups chicken (or vegan chicken-flavor) broth
- ⅓ cup lemon juice
- ½ cup olive oil
- 1½ tsp kosher salt

For the filling:

- 2 cups jasmine rice
- 4 oz ground beef or ground vegan meat
- 1 cup chopped cilantro or flat-leaf parsley
- 2 Tbsp tomato paste
- 1 Tbsp tamarind sauce
- 2 tsp kosher salt
- pulp from tomatoes, for stuffing

DIRECTIONS

1. Soak rice in cold water for 1 hour. Set aside.

2. Cut the very top and the bottom of each onion and peel the rough skin. With a sharp knife, make a slit lengthwise halfway through the onion, until you reach the core. Put the onions in a large pot and cover with cold, salted water. Bring to boil over high heat, reduce the heat, cover the pan and cook for 10 minutes. Drain and cover the onions in cold water, then let cool until easy to handle, about 20 minutes.

3. When the onions have cooled down, separate them into layers and put the layers in a large bowl.

4. Use a serrated knife to remove the top of the tomatoes, like a lid. Use a spoon to scoop out the pulp and seeds. Lightly salt the inside. Keep pulp for later.

5. Strain the rice and mix with ground beef, cilantro, tomato paste, tamarind and salt. Chop tomato pulp and add to the mixture. Mix well.

6. Spray a 12-14 inch round pan with oil. Stuff tomatoes with rice mixture ¾ of the way and place in the center of the pan. Add a couple of spoonfuls of the filling to each onion layer, and roll it back over the filling. Arrange tightly in the pan around the tomatoes.

7. Put chicken broth, lemon juice, olive oil and salt in a small pot and bring to boil. Pour gently over the stuffed onions and tomatoes in the pan. Make sure the tomatoes are filled with the sauce, you can use a spoon to fill them.

8. Put the pan over medium-high heat and bring to boil. Reduce the heat to low, cover the pan and cook on a very low simmer for 1½ hours. Check from time to time to see that the onion bottoms are not too charred. You do want them to get dark brown, but not burnt. Remove the lid and cook for ½ hour longer, until the sauce has thickened and the onions are caramelized at the bottom. Cover again, and let sit for 30-60 minutes before serving.

SABICH

YIELD: 4 SERVINGS

SABICH

Mike Solomonov

Sabich is one of the most popular street foods in Israel, originating from the Iraqi Jewish community. Sabich is composed of thinly sliced fried eggplant, hard-boiled egg (or slow-cooked huevos haminados) and tahini, though it can also include chopped salad, pickles, amba and more. The combination of slow-cooked eggs, eggplant, potato and amba was the classic Shabbat morning breakfast for Jews of Iraq, since all of these items could be eaten at room temperature.

When the Iraqi Jews moved to Israel, primarily in the 1950s, they continued eating their standard Shabbat breakfast. But, following a wider trend in Israeli society at the time, someone had the idea to stuff the traditional breakfast into a pita pocket, thus turning it into an informal sandwich, which quickly became popular.

Note: *You will need to make the huevos haminados ahead of time; they cook for 8-12 hours.*

INGREDIENTS

For the huevos haminados (slow-cooked eggs):

- 6 large eggs
- 2 black tea bags
- 2 Tbsp Turkish coffee

For the fried eggplant:

- 1 large eggplant
- 4 Tbsp kosher salt
- ½ cup cornstarch
- canola oil, for frying

- peels from 4 onions
- 2 quarts water

To serve:

- tahini sauce (see page 10)
- amba sauce (see page 14)
- pita bread (see page 54)

DIRECTIONS

1. To make the huevos haminados: Preheat the oven to 200°F. Mix all the ingredients with the water in a large ovenproof pot. Cover and bake for at least 8 hours, or up to 12 hours.

2. Remove the pot from the oven. Crack, but do not peel, the eggs, then return them to the pot with the liquid. Set the pot on the stovetop and cook over high heat, uncovered, until almost all the liquid has evaporated, about 20 minutes (watch closely, the eggs will explode if the pot gets too dry). Cool the eggs on a plate, then peel and slice.

3. To make the fried eggplant: Stripe the eggplant lengthwise with a vegetable peeler and trim off the ends. Slice into 12 roughly ½-inch-thick rounds. Sprinkle each of the eggplant slices on both sides with the salt and drain on a wire rack set on a baking sheet for 1 hour.

4. Pat the slices dry with paper towels. Put the cornstarch in a shallow bowl. Dredge the eggplant in the cornstarch on both sides and tap off the excess. Place a large skillet over medium heat and coat the bottom with oil. When the oil is hot, fry the eggplant in batches for about 2 minutes per side, or until golden. With a spatula, transfer the eggplant to paper towels to drain. Cool slightly before assembly.

5. Assemble ingredients into a fresh pita and drizzle with amba and tahini.

SCHNITZEL

YIELD: 4-6 SERVINGS

SCHNITZEL

The Nosher Staff

*Schnitzel did not start out as an Israeli dish, but rather originated as Viennese Wiener schnitzel —
a breaded, pan-fried veal cutlet. The Israeli version, made with turkey or chicken, was introduced
by immigrants from Central Europe decades before the country was even established. In "The
Encyclopedia of Jewish Food," Gil Marks attributes the popularity of poultry schnitzel to a
program run by the Ministry of Absorption in the 1940s, which taught housewives how to prepare
simple recipes with easily accessible, cheap ingredients. Schnitzel has since become one of
Israel's most common, everyday dishes: every butcher in Israel carries the "schnitzel" cut (thinly
sliced or pounded chicken breast), and you can find schnitzel everywhere — from the freezer
section of supermarkets to gas stations to markets.*

INGREDIENTS

- 2 eggs, lightly beaten
- 2 heaping Tbsp good-quality mustard
- 3-4 garlic cloves, smashed
- freshly ground pepper
- 2 cups unseasoned bread crumbs

For serving:

- 3-4 lemons, halved

- 2 lb boneless chicken breast, very thinly pounded
- 2 Tbsp sesame seeds
- freshly ground pepper and sea salt
- canola oil, for frying

DIRECTIONS

1. Combine eggs, mustard, garlic and pepper in a large bowl. Add the chicken and mix until it's completely coated. Cover with plastic wrap and refrigerate for at least 2 hours, preferably overnight.

2. Remove the chicken from the refrigerator and let sit at room temperature for 20 minutes. Meanwhile, in a shallow bowl, mix together the bread crumbs and sesame seeds. Season with freshly ground pepper and sea salt.

3. Dredge chicken breasts in bread crumbs, patting slightly to help them stick.

4. Pour oil into a medium skillet to about 1½ inches high. Heat oil on high heat until very hot and add chicken breasts, just 2-3 at a time (depending on their size). Do not overcrowd the skillet. Reduce heat to medium, and fry the chicken until golden brown on each side and completely cooked through. Repeat with remaining chicken.

5. Remove chicken from the pan with a slotted spoon and place on a serving plate lined with paper towels until all chicken is fried.

6. Serve immediately with fresh lemon if desired.

SHAKSHUKA

Photo: Doug Schneider

YIELD: 2-4 SERVINGS

SHAKSHUKA

Shannon Sarna

Shakshuka is a North African dish made from tomatoes, peppers, spices and eggs that are simmered in the sauce. Brought to Israel by Libyan and other Northern African Jewish immigrants, the exact origin of the dish is unknown but shakshuka has become one of the most popular dishes throughout Israel.

INGREDIENTS

- 2-3 Tbsp olive oil
- 1 large onion, finely chopped
- 1 jalapeño or other hot pepper, seeded and finely diced
- 1 roasted red pepper, chopped
- 3 garlic cloves, minced
- 1 Tbsp tomato paste
- 2-3 Tbsp harissa paste (optional)
- 1 Tbsp paprika
- 1 tsp ground cumin
- ¼ tsp caraway seeds
- 1 28-oz can diced tomatoes
- 1 tsp salt
- ½ tsp freshly ground black pepper
- ½-1 cup water or vegetable stock (optional)
- 3-4 large eggs
- fresh parsley, mint and/or cilantro (optional)

DIRECTIONS

1. Heat the oil in a large sauté pan over medium heat.

2. Add the onion and cook until translucent, 5-7 minutes. Add the jalapeño, garlic and roasted red pepper and cook for another 2 minutes. Add the tomato paste, harissa, paprika, cumin and caraway seeds and continue to cook for 3-4 minutes, until fragrant.

3. Add the diced tomatoes, salt and black pepper and simmer over medium heat for 15-20 minutes. If you prefer the sauce a little thinner, add ½-1 cup of water or vegetable stock.

4. When the sauce has reached your desired consistency, crack each egg, one at a time, into a small glass bowl and then gently add to the tomato sauce. Cover and cook for 3-5 minutes, until the whites have set and the yolks are to your liking.

5. Sprinkle with fresh herbs (if using) before serving.

PASHTIDA

Photo: Emanuelle Lee

YIELD: 2-4 SERVINGS

PASHTIDA

Emanuelle Lee

Pashtida (a crustless quiche) is beloved and common in Israel, where it is enjoyed at potlucks, school events, shivas and everything in-between. It's also commonly prepared for Shavuot and Sukkot. This versatile dish transports well, and there is no right or wrong way to make it. Israelis make pashtida all year long, but it's a dish that's especially perfect for warmer climates and seasons, when it's just too hot to spend hours in an overheated kitchen. Plus, during warmer months, there are so many incredible seasonal ingredients available to include in the pashtida, making it extra delicious. You should feel free to use this recipe as a base and add the vegetables and cheese that speak most to your taste.

INGREDIENTS

- 2 Tbsp + 1 tsp olive oil
- 6 scallions, roughly chopped
- 2 zucchinis, sliced into thin rounds
- 2 ears of corn, kernels removed from cob
- 2½ cups cherry or grape tomatoes, half of them cut in half
- 4 eggs
- 3 Tbsp all-purpose flour
- ⅓ cup ricotta
- 3½ oz fresh mozzarella
- 2 oz cheddar cheese, grated
- 1 Tbsp butter
- 1 large handful fresh basil
- sea salt and black pepper

DIRECTIONS

1. Preheat the oven to 350°F.

2. Stand the ears of corn up on a plate and carefully remove the kernels by cutting downward with a sharp knife.

3. Heat a medium-large pan on high heat and add the corn kernels to the dry pan. Stir occasionally, allowing them to become bright yellow in color and a little bit charred. Transfer the corn to another plate, season with a pinch of sea salt and allow half of the butter to melt over it.

4. Let the pan cool for a few minutes and then place it back onto medium heat. Add 1 Tbsp olive oil and then add the zucchini slices. Stir occasionally, until they become slightly softened and begin to brown. Transfer to the plate with the corn and add the remaining butter and a pinch of sea salt.

5. Wipe the pan with a paper towel. Over medium heat, heat 1 tsp olive oil and add the scallions. They should sizzle and become charred within a few minutes. Stir them occasionally, then remove them from the pan.

6. Add the last Tbsp of olive oil to the pan along with the tomatoes. Let them blister and soften slightly. Season with a pinch of salt and remove them from the heat. Allow all the cooked vegetables to cool down.

7. In a mixing bowl, beat the eggs until slightly frothy. Slowly add the flour and mix continuously. Then add the ricotta and mix well. Season with a pinch of salt and black pepper.

8. Add the vegetables into the egg mixture, reserving a little bit of each vegetable for the top. Mix well. Shred half of the mozzarella into small pieces and add to the mixture.

9. Lightly grease an 8-inch round cake tin or pie dish with butter or olive oil. Sprinkle half of the grated cheddar around the bottom and sides of the tin or dish. Pour the mixture into the tin or dish. Shred the remainder of the mozzarella over the top of the mixture and then top with the remaining grated cheddar. Season with a pinch of salt and pepper, and top with the reserved vegetables.

10. Bake the pashtida for 30-35 minutes, or until it's fluffy and cooked through.

ISRAELI COUSCOUS PILAF   Photo: Lynda Balslev

YIELD: 2-4 SERVINGS

ISRAELI COUSCOUS PILAF

Lynda Balslev

Unlike the finely grained North African couscous made of semolina, Israeli couscous has larger granules resembling tiny pearls, which are made of baked wheat. The result is a pasta-like product, which remains firm when cooked and has a delicious toasted-wheat flavor, similar to the Sardinian pasta fregola sarda. Because of its shape and size, Israeli couscous is sometimes marketed as "pearl couscous." Yet in Israel, it goes by neither of these names — it's called ptitim, which means "flakes" in Hebrew.

Ptitim's origin is relatively modern, and was integral to the early days of Israel. Following the War of Independence, when the country was newly formed and faced rationing, Prime Minister David Ben-Gurion tasked Osem, one of Israel's largest food manufacturers and distributors, with creating an inexpensive starch that was more affordable than pricey rice. The result was an extruded wheat paste in the form of rice granules that were dried and toasted. This product quickly became a family staple. Over time, the shapes evolved, including into small pearl shapes resembling maftoul, the hand-rolled Palestinian couscous made from bulgur wheat.

In this recipe, ptitim are cooked pilaf-style, flavored with warm spices and strewn with pine nuts, currants and fresh mint before serving. Serve with grilled meat or chicken for a light summer dinner.

INGREDIENTS

- 1¼ cups chicken stock
- ½ tsp sea salt
- ¼ tsp ground cardamom
- pinch ground cinnamon
- generous pinch saffron threads
- 1 Tbsp olive oil

- ¼ cup yellow onion, finely chopped
- 1 cup Israeli couscous
- 2 Tbsp pine nuts, toasted
- 2 Tbsp currants
- 2 Tbsp mint, finely chopped

DIRECTIONS

1. Combine the stock, salt, cardamom, cinnamon and saffron in a small saucepan and bring to a simmer over medium heat.

2. Heat the oil in a large saucepan over medium heat. Add the onion and sauté until softened without coloring, about 2 minutes. Add the Israeli couscous and cook, stirring, until lightly toasted, about 1 minute.

3. Carefully add the stock to the pan and stir to combine. Cover the pan and simmer over medium-low heat until the liquid has been absorbed and the couscous is tender, 8-10 minutes. Remove the pan from the heat, remove the lid and fluff the couscous with a fork. Lay a clean dish towel over the pan (without touching the couscous) and place the lid over the towel. Let stand for 5 minutes to allow the towel to absorb the steam.

4. Stir in the pine nuts, currants and mint. Serve warm or at room temperature.

CHRAIMEH

Photo: Vered Guttman

YIELD: 4 SERVINGS

CHRAIMEH

Vered Guttman

Chraimeh is a classic Tunisian dish, and a favorite among Israelis of all origins. This dish is served on many holiday tables; you can think of it as a Mizrahi replacement for gefilte fish. Traditionally, the fish is cut into steaks as the skin and bones add flavor to the sauce, though you can also use fish fillet, if you prefer. Any firm fish can work here, even salmon. In Israel the preferred fish is carp.

INGREDIENTS

- ⅓ cup corn oil, safflower oil or mild olive oil, plus more for frying
- 12 garlic cloves, chopped
- 2 Tbsp paprika
- 1 tsp caraway seeds
- chili pepper flakes, to taste
- kosher salt

- 3 Tbsp tomato paste
- 1 tsp sugar
- 1⅓ cups water, at room temperature
- 4 fish steaks, such as salmon, tilapia or red snapper
- ½ tsp white pepper

For serving:

- 4 Serrano peppers (optional)
- 1 lemon

- ¼ cup chopped cilantro

DIRECTIONS

1. Place a wide pan (that can hold all the fish in one layer) on medium heat. Add oil. When the oil is hot, add garlic and sauté until garlic is transparent, stirring frequently, about 2 minutes.

2. Add paprika, caraway seeds, chili flakes and 1½ tsp salt, and cook for 1 minute.

3. Add tomato paste, mix and cook for 1 minute.

4. Add water, mix, bring to a boil, cover, reduce heat to low and simmer for 5 minutes.

5. Add the fish in one layer, sprinkle with a little salt and white pepper, and drizzle some of the sauce over the top. Cover the pan and cook on a low simmer for 10-15 minutes until the fish is fully cooked (it depends on the thickness of the fish). Let fish stand in the covered pan for 5 minutes before serving.

6. While the fish is cooking, fry whole Serrano peppers in a little oil in a small pan over medium-high heat until tender and a little charred. Set aside.

7. Transfer fish and sauce to serving plates. Drizzle with lemon juice, sprinkle with cilantro and serve with one Serrano pepper per person on the side.

KTZITZOT PRASA   Photo: Danielle Oron

YIELD: 4-6 SERVINGS

KTZITZOT PRASA

Danielle Oron

Leeks are a traditional and significant ingredient in Sephardi cooking, and can be found in dishes for Rosh Hashanah, Hanukkah, Passover and other holidays. These ktzitzot prasa, or leek patties, are crispy on the outside and soft on the inside. Boiling the leeks for five minutes mellows out the flavor and softens them up. If you would like to make a vegetarian version, you can leave out the beef completely. (There is no need to substitute with any other ingredients.)

INGREDIENTS

For the dipping sauce:

- ⅓ cup mayo
- 1½ Tbsp lemon juice

- 1½ tsp zhug (store-bought is totally fine or see page 12)

For the fritters:

- 1 medium russet potato, peeled and cut into 1-inch pieces
- 4-5 medium leeks, white and light green parts cut in half lengthwise and sliced into ½-inch half-rounds
- ¼ lb ground beef
- ⅓ cup matzah meal

- 1 large egg
- 1 tsp kosher salt
- 1½ tsp ground cumin
- freshly ground black pepper
- canola oil, for frying
- lemon wedges, to serve

DIRECTIONS

1. To make the dipping sauce: In a small bowl, combine the mayo, lemon juice and zhug. Cover and set in the fridge until ready to serve.

2. To make the fritters: Start by placing potatoes in a medium pot and cover with at least 4 cups cold water. Bring to a boil over high heat.

3. Boil the potatoes for 8 minutes then add the leeks. Boil for an additional 5 minutes then drain into a colander. Allow to cool for 15 minutes.

4. Find the potato pieces and transfer to a large bowl. Mash the potato with a fork until smooth.

5. Add the leeks, beef, matzah meal, egg, salt, cumin and fresh black pepper. Mix with your hands until well combined.

6. Using wet hands, take about 2 Tbsp of mixture and shape into patties.

7. In a large non-stick skillet or pan, add enough canola oil to cover the bottom of the pan by ½ inch. Heat over medium heat until the oil shimmers.

8. Once oil is hot, fry patties in batches for 2-3 minutes on the first side then 1-2 minutes on the second side. Transfer to a cooling rack to ensure they stay crispy, and sprinkle them with a bit of kosher salt.

9. Serve with lots of lemon wedges and dipping sauce.

CHICKEN SHAWARMA KEBAB

Photo: Chaya Rapaport

YIELD: 4 SERVINGS

CHICKEN SHAWARMA KEBAB

Chaya Rapaport

In Israel, kebabs of spiced ground meat or chicken thighs (pargiyot) are ubiquitous at holiday barbecues. These juicy chicken thigh kebabs are inspired by the flavorings of one of the country's most beloved street foods: shawarma. Marinated in classic shawarma spices like cumin, turmeric and coriander, unlike spit-roasted shawarma, these kebabs take mere minutes to cook on a hot grill (you could do this on a grill pan, too).

Serve in warm laffa — a flatbread favored by greedy Israelis, as it holds more than the smaller pita — with fresh hummus, brightened with sliced red onion.

INGREDIENTS

For the kebabs:

- 4-5 4 oz skinless, boneless chicken thighs, trimmed of excess fat and cut into ½-inch cubes
- ¼ cup olive oil
- 1½ tsp ground cumin
- 1 tsp ground black pepper

- 1 tsp ground turmeric
- 1 tsp sea salt
- ½ tsp smoked paprika
- ¾ tsp garlic powder
- ¾ tsp ground coriander

To serve:

- parsley
- thinly sliced red onion

- hummus
- laffa bread

DIRECTIONS

1. Combine the spices in a bowl. Add the cubed chicken and olive oil, and mix well to combine. Cover and refrigerate for a minimum of 30 minutes, and up to 12 hours. The longer it marinates, the tastier it'll be!

2. Take 12-15 wooden or metal skewers. If you're using wooden skewers, soak them for 30 minutes so they don't burn and catch fire on the grill. Thread the marinated chicken onto the skewers — I like to thread them longways so there's more surface area to grill.

3. Preheat the grill to medium-high heat and grease it by dipping a few paper towels in vegetable oil then, using tongs, rub them carefully over the grates until glossy.

4. Place the kebabs on the grill and cook until golden brown, around 5-6 minutes per side. Use tongs to turn them. They should be charred in places.

5. Transfer to a platter and scatter with parsley and sliced red onion. Serve with warm laffa bread and hummus.

ROASTED VEGETABLES WITH TAHINI

Photo: Rachel Simons

ROASTED VEGETABLES WITH TAHINI

Rachel Simons

In Israel, and increasingly in Israeli and Middle Eastern restaurants abroad, it's common to find roasted cauliflower smothered in tahini sauce, an irresistible combination popularized by celebrity chef Eyal Shani over a decade ago. In this recipe, you can use any combination of vegetables you have on hand or prefer, but a whole cauliflower head makes a striking centerpiece.

INGREDIENTS

- 1 head cauliflower
- 1 red onion
- shishito peppers
- whole carrots
- 5 Tbsp olive oil

- pomegranate wedges, for garnish (optional)
- fresh parsley, for garnish (optional)
- tahini sauce, for serving (see page 10)

DIRECTIONS

1. Preheat the oven to 400°F.

2. Place the whole head of cauliflower in a pot of boiling water for 7 minutes. Remove and pat dry. Place the cauliflower head and all other selected vegetables on a parchment-lined sheet pan. Drizzle with roughly 5 Tbsp olive oil and season with salt and pepper. Roast for 45 minutes or until browned.

3. Place the vegetables on a platter with the whole cauliflower as the centerpiece and drizzle with tahini sauce. Garnish with wedges of pomegranate and parsley for extra color, if desired.

KREMBOS

Photo: Micah Siva

Desserts

- HALVA SWIRL BROWNIES

- ISRAELI ICEBOX CAKE

- KREMBOS

- PULL-APART RUGELACH CAKE

- ROLLED MA'MOUL COOKIES

- FROZEN LIMONANA

HALVA SWIRL BROWNIES   Photo: Jamie Vespa

YIELD: 8-10 SERVINGS

HALVA SWIRL BROWNIES

Shannon Sarna

In Israel, you find halva and tahini incorporated into many sweets: as a babka filling, added to cookie dough, and used as a topping for ice cream. Chocolate and halva are a particularly perfect flavor combination. In this brownie recipe, halva and cream cheese are combined for a creamy, tart swirled fudgy treat, and more crumbled halva gets added on top.

INGREDIENTS

For the halva-cream-cheese layer:

- 5 oz cream cheese, at room temperature
- 2 Tbsp butter, softened
- ¼ cup granulated sugar
- 1 egg
- 1 Tbsp flour
- ½ cup tahini

For the brownie layer:

- ¾ cups flour
- ⅓ cup Hershey's Special Dark Cocoa
- ½ tsp baking powder
- ¼ tsp cinnamon
- ½ tsp salt
- ¼ cup (½ stick) butter, softened
- 1 cup sugar
- 1 tsp vanilla
- 2 large eggs
- ¼ cup chocolate chips

For the top:

- ¼–½ cup crumbled halva pieces

DIRECTIONS

1. Preheat the oven to 350°F. Grease and line an 8x8 baking pan with cooking spray.

2. To make the brownie layer: Sift flour, cocoa, cinnamon, salt and baking powder into a medium-sized bowl. In a small bowl, cream the sugar and butter together until smooth, add eggs one at a time, beat well, then add vanilla. Fold egg, sugar, butter and vanilla mixture into the bowl of dry ingredients. Fold in chocolate chips. Spread ¾ of the brownie batter into the bottom of the lined baking pan.

3. To make the cream-cheese-tahini layer: Using a hand mixer or stand mixer, cream together butter, sugar and flour. Add cream cheese and mix until smooth.

4. Scrape bowl and add the egg and beat until light and creamy. Scrape down the bowl again and add the tahini. Beat 1 minute or until the tahini is mixed into the cream cheese mixture completely.

5. To assemble: Randomly dollop the tahini-cream-cheese topping over the brownie batter. Dollop the remaining brownie batter on top.

6. Sprinkle halva pieces on top. Swirl the topping into batter using a butter knife.

7. Bake for around 40-45 minutes. Allow to cool and cut brownies into squares.

ISRAELI ICEBOX CAKE   Photo: Sonya Sanford

YIELD: 12-16 SERVINGS

ISRAELI ICEBOX CAKE

Sonya Sanford

One of Israel's best-loved desserts is a no-bake cake made with tea biscuits. Israeli biscuit cake (ugat bisquivitim in Hebrew) is Israel's version of an icebox cake or tiramisu. It's designed to be thrown together on a whim, with simple products found in most kitchens.

Many recipes call for gvina levana, a white cheese called "quark" in the States and Europe. Quark is a fresh dairy product that tastes like a cross between sour cream and Greek yogurt, and adds a delicious tanginess to the filling. Instant vanilla pudding offers its unmistakable flavor and helps the cake set in the fridge. While it's in the fridge, this cake transforms from a loose, creamy consistency into a sliceable layered cake.

INGREDIENTS

- 3 sleeves (238 g/9 oz) Kedem vanilla tea biscuits or 2 sleeves Osem petit beurre biscuits
- 2 cups heavy whipping cream
- 1 cup milk
- 1 (80 g/2.8 oz) packet instant vanilla pudding mix (or 5 Tbsp)
- ¼ cup sugar
- ¼ tsp salt
- 1 cup (250 g/8 oz) quark or 5% Greek yogurt
- 2 tsp vanilla extract
- 1 cup cold coffee or milk
- chocolate, for garnish (optional)

DIRECTIONS

1. In a large bowl using a handheld mixer or whisk, beat together the heavy cream, milk, instant vanilla pudding mix, sugar and salt until the mixture starts to thicken and the mixer or whisk leaves ribbons in the batter, about 2-3 minutes. Be careful not to overbeat the mixture.

2. Add the quark and vanilla extract, and beat until just combined.

3. To assemble, dip one tea biscuit at a time into the coffee or milk for 2-3 seconds (if using Osem tea biscuits, dip for a few seconds longer). Line the bottom of a 9x13 inch baking pan with the dipped tea biscuits. Cut any biscuits to fit the pan as needed. Top the layer of biscuits with a third of the filling.

4. Repeat the process twice until you have three layers of tea biscuits and three of filling.

5. To garnish, top with milk or dark chocolate shavings; you can do this with a vegetable peeler and a bar of chocolate. Alternatively, you could also top with cocoa powder or sprinkles.

6. Cover the baking dish tightly with plastic wrap and refrigerate overnight or for at least 6 hours. Cut into slices and serve cold.

KREMBOS

Photo: Micah Siva

KREMBOS

Micah Siva

Krembos — chocolate-coated domes of whipped marshmallow on a cookie base — are Israel's favorite confection. The foil-wrapped seasonal treats are only available in the colder months, and "krembo season" is always highly anticipated by local kids (and adults!). This recipe elevates the store-bought treat, with a buttery cookie base topped with a swirl of lighter-than-air marshmallow cream and coated in a thin layer of chocolate. They provide the perfect balance of textures.

Note: *You can make the cookie base one to two days in advance, if necessary. The finished krembos can be stored in an airtight container for up to two days. They also freeze well.*

INGREDIENTS

For the cookie base:

- ½ cup unsalted butter or vegan butter
- ⅓ cup powdered sugar
- 1 egg yolk
- 1 Tbsp vanilla extract
- ½ tsp sea salt
- 1⅓ cup flour
- 1-2 Tbsp water, as needed

For the marshmallow cream:

- ¾ cups sugar
- ½ cup water
- 3 large egg whites, at room temperature
- ¼ tsp cream of tartar
- 1 Tbsp vanilla

For the chocolate shell:

- 1 cup chocolate chips
- ½ cup coconut oil

DIRECTIONS

1. To make the cookie base: Combine the butter and powdered sugar with a stand or hand mixer until fluffy. Add the egg yolk, vanilla extract and sea salt until combined. Add the flour and 1-2 Tbsp water as needed, until a crumbly dough forms.

2. Shape into a disc, cover and refrigerate for at least 20 minutes or overnight.

3. Preheat the oven to 350°F. Line a baking tray with parchment paper.

4. On a lightly floured surface, roll the dough to ¼-inch thickness. Cut 2½-inch circles out of the dough, then re-roll the scraps to cut more circles. Transfer to the baking tray and refrigerate for 10 minutes.

5. Bake for 11-13 minutes, or until golden.

6. Transfer to a cooling rack until they cool to room temperature.

7. To make the marshmallow cream: In a small saucepan, heat the sugar and water to 240°F over medium heat. Once the sugar mixture reaches 200°F, begin whipping the egg whites and cream of tartar in a stand mixer to stiff peaks.

8. Once the sugar mixture reaches 240°F, pour the sugar syrup into the whipping egg whites, beating on high for 5-7 minutes, or until stable and shiny.

9. Transfer to a piping bag fitted with a large, round tip. Holding the piping bag vertically, pipe a tall mound on each cookie. Transfer to the fridge until set.

10. To make the chocolate shell: Melt the chocolate in a double boiler (or in the microwave in 30-second increments). Add the coconut oil, mixing to combine. It should be the consistency of heavy cream.

11. Spoon the chocolate coating over the marshmallow. Return to the fridge to set.

PULL-APART RUGELACH CAKE

Photo: Lior Maschiach

YIELD: 4-6 SERVINGS

PULL-APART RUGELACH CAKE

Lior Maschiach

Israeli rugelach are quite different from the American version. Instead of a cream cheese and butter dough, which is chilled then rolled out, Israeli rugelach are made from a yeasted dough, which is spread with chocolate or other fillings, rolled and baked. After they are baked, a simple syrup is often brushed on top, adding to the sweetness, sheen and gooey texture. This cake layers flaky Israeli rugelach on top of one another in a round pan, creating an irresistible pull-apart rugelach "cake."

INGREDIENTS

For the dough:

- 3 tsp (13 g) active dry yeast
- 1 cup (250 ml) whole milk, at room temperature
- 3½ Tbsp (40 g) sugar
- ⅓ cup (80 g) butter, melted
- 4 cups (500 g) bread flour
- pinch of salt
- 2 Tbsp ground cardamom
- 1 egg + 1 beaten egg, for brushing

For the filling:

- ⅔ cup (160 g) butter, softened
- ¾ cup (80 g) cocoa
- 1⅓ cups (160 g) powdered sugar
- 3.5 oz (100 g) cookie crumbs
- a pinch of salt

- ½ cup Nutella or hazelnut-chocolate spread
- 1 tsp vanilla extract

For the syrup:

- 1 cup (200 g) granulated sugar
- ⅓ cup + 4 tsp (100 g) water

DIRECTIONS

1. Place the yeast and milk in the bowl of a stand mixer fitted with the dough hook attachment and mix well. Add the sugar and melted butter, and mix.

2. Add the salt and ground cardamom to the flour and mix. Gradually, while continuously kneading with the dough hook, add the flour mixture to the mixer. It's possible, depending on the time of year and the climate where you live, that you may not need to use all the flour — the dough shouldn't be too wet or too dry. Look for a soft, smooth texture.

3. Add the egg and knead until the dough separates from the bowl.

4. Transfer the dough to a greased bowl, cover and let rise for 30 minutes.

5. For the filling, place all the ingredients in a bowl and mix well. Set aside at room temperature until ready to use. The filling should have a spreadable consistency; if it is too cold it will tear the dough when spread, and if it's too soft it will melt.

6. To assemble the rugelach, line an 8 or 9 inch round baking pan with parchment paper. Place the dough on a lightly floured work surface and roll to a 40x40 cm/16x16 inch rectangle, about 5 mm/0.2 inch thick. Spread an even layer of the filling all the way to the edges.

7. Fold the dough into thirds, as you would fold a letter: Grab the top edge and fold it toward the center, and then grab the bottom edge and fold it over to cover. Roll to a 20x40 cm/8x16 inch rectangle, 5 mm/0.2 inch thick.

8. Using a pizza cutter, cut the dough in half, so you have two rectangular strips 10x40 cm/4x16 inches. Make a notch every 6 cm/2.5 inches along one side of each strip, and use that marking to cut to triangles.

9. Cut a small slit at the wide end of the triangle, then tightly roll up into a crescent shape, making sure the tip is underneath.

10. Place the rugelach in the baking pan, overlapping one another. Cover, and let rise for 45-60 minutes.

11. Preheat the oven to 180°C/350°F.

12. Bake for 20-25 minutes until golden brown.

13. While the cake is baking, prepare the syrup by placing the sugar and water in a saucepan. Bring to a boil until sugar is dissolved, then set aside.

14. Brush the rugelach cake with the hot syrup as soon as it comes out of the oven. Allow to cool before serving.

ROLLED MA'MOUL COOKIES   Photo: Shlomo Schwartz

YIELD: 2 DOZEN COOKIES

ROLLED MA'MOUL COOKIES

Shlomo Schwartz

Ma'amoul is a traditional small pastry stuffed with dates and walnuts from the Levant. Muslims, Christians and Jews lived in this area alongside each other for over 1,500 years. Among the many cultural and culinary traditions they share are the intricately decorated and delicious ma'amoul. Traditionally, these cookies are formed using a decorated wooden mold, which can be a labor of love. Many Israelis today make an easier version of the treat stuffed with date spread and walnuts, but also chocolate spread and other fillings. This version is filled with date spread, chopped pecans and halva, but you can just use date and walnuts if you prefer a more classic cookie.

***Note:** Date spread can be found at Middle Eastern or kosher markets. Date spread is different from date paste.*

INGREDIENTS

For the dough:

- 3½ cups flour
- 10.5 oz butter or margarine, at room temperature
- 2 tsp baking powder

For the filling:

- 1½ cup date spread
- 4 oz crumbled halva
- ¾ cup chopped, roasted pecans

- 2 tsp vanilla sugar
- ½ cup water, at room temperature
- zest of 1 lemon

To serve:

- confectioner's sugar

DIRECTIONS

1. Preheat the oven to 340°F. Prep a baking sheet with parchment paper.

2. In a large bowl, use your hands to mix all of the dough ingredients until fully combined. You can use a mixer with a dough hook attachment if you prefer. Cut into two portions.

3. On a lightly floured surface, roll one portion of the dough into a ½-inch-thick rectangle. Trim the edges to refine the rectangle.

4. Spread half of the date spread evenly onto the dough and sprinkle half of the halvah and pecans on top.

5. Carefully roll the dough tightly, starting from the side that is closer to you, and place the seam-side down on the prepared baking sheet. Using your fingers, pinch the ends of the log to seal. Repeat the same steps with the second half of the dough, and then bake in the preheated oven for 35 minutes.

6. Remove from the oven and cool for about 10-15 minutes.

7. Once the dough slightly cools, carefully slice the logs into 1-inch slices using a large knife. (Prevent the dough from crumbling by using a knife that's not serrated.)

8. Let the sliced ma'amoul cool completely, and sprinkle with a generous amount of confectioner's sugar before serving.

FROZEN LIMONANA

Photo: Chaya Rapaport

FROZEN LIMONANA
Chaya Rapaport

Limonana is a classic Israeli-style lemonade that combines freshly squeezed lemon juice and mint leaves. Limonana is a combination of the Hebrew and Arabic words "limon" and "nana," which mean lemon and mint, respectively. While the drink may have originated elsewhere in the Middle East, it's an Israeli advertising agency that gave it its catchy portmanteau of a name in the 1990s — and the drink is beloved nationwide. It's common to find regular limonana at cafes as well as this frozen version, which doubles as a refreshing summer treat or the perfect base for a summer cocktail: just add tequila, vodka, arak or spirit of choice.

INGREDIENTS

- ¾ cup freshly squeezed lemon juice, from around 3 lemons
- ½ cup loosely packed mint leaves
- 6 Tbsp sugar
- 1 cup water
- 4 cups ice cubes

DIRECTIONS

1. Combine water, sugar and half of the mint leaves in a small saucepan. Bring to a boil, stirring until sugar dissolves. Simmer for 1 minute.

2. Remove from heat and let syrup steep, about 30 minutes. Discard the mint leaves and refrigerate the syrup to let it cool.

3. Combine the mint simple syrup, the rest of the fresh mint leaves and the fresh lemon juice in a blender. Blend at high speed until well mixed.

4. Add the ice and blend until the ice is thoroughly crushed. Pour into glasses and serve immediately.

KUBANEH

Photo: Lior Mashiach

Breads

- FLUFFY PITA BREAD
- YEMENITE KUBANEH BREAD

PITA BREAD

Photo: Shannon Sarna

PITA BREAD

YIELD: 6-8 PITAS

FLUFFY PITA BREAD

Shannon Sarna

Once you make your own pita bread, you will never go back to store-bought. It's a relatively quick bread to make from scratch, since it only requires around two hours of rising. And there is nothing quite as gratifying as watching the pita rise in the oven and puff up to form its coveted pocket.

A few tips on how to make pita that will puff every time:
• Preheat your oven for a long time before baking.
• Use a pizza stone if you have one, and preheat the stone. If you don't have a pizza stone, use a baking sheet — but make sure to preheat the baking sheet.
• Use a rolling pin to roll out each piece before popping into the oven.

INGREDIENTS

- 2 tsp yeast
- ½ tsp sugar
- 1 cup + 3 Tbsp lukewarm water
- 3 cups unbleached all-purpose flour
- 2 Tbsp olive oil
- 2 tsp salt

DIRECTIONS

1. Combine yeast, sugar and water. Allow to proof for 5 minutes.

2. In a mixer fitted with the dough hook attachment, add the flour, olive oil and salt. Add the yeast-water mixture and mix on low until the dough comes together. Raise the mixer speed to medium and mix for 3-5 minutes. If dough seems too dry, add water 1 Tbsp at a time, taking care not to add too much water. If it feels too loose and wet, add an additional 1 Tbsp flour. The dough should be firm, slightly shiny and bounce back slightly when you touch it.

3. Allow dough to rise in a greased bowl for 2 hours with a towel draped on top or covered in plastic wrap. (Note: You can do a slower rise overnight in the fridge.)

4. Preheat the oven to 500°F and place the pizza stone on the top rack of the oven to heat. Leave the pizza stone in the heated oven for at least 30 minutes. (Please check your pizza stone's maximum temperature. Some pizza stones can only withstand a 400°F oven.)

5. Divide the dough into 6-8 even pieces (use a food scale to measure most precisely).

6. Roll each piece into a smooth ball and place on a baking sheet lined with parchment paper or a silicone baking mat. Drape a towel over the baking sheet and allow to sit for another 30 minutes.

7. Using a rolling pin, roll out each piece of dough into a flat, round disc, around 3 inches wide and ½ inch thick. Keep remaining balls of dough covered while you are working.

8. In batches of one or two, place a flattened disc on a pizza stone at the back of the oven. Watching closely, bake for 3 minutes or until the pita has puffed up. Flip onto the other side and bake for another 30-60 seconds.

9. Using metal tongs, remove pita from the oven and wrap immediately in a towel. Repeat with remaining dough until all the pitas have baked. Keep the pita wrapped in a towel until it has completely cooled. If you place still-warm pita in a plastic bag or container, condensation will form and the bread will get soggy.

KUBANEH

Photo: Lior Maschiach

YIELD: 4-6 SERVINGS

YEMENITE KUBANEH BREAD

Lior Maschiach

Kubaneh is a uniquely Yemenite Jewish bread that is traditionally slowly baked in a tall, round pan overnight, from Friday to Saturday, to enjoy on Shabbat morning. Yemenite Jewish immigrants brought it to Israel, where it has gained considerable popularity. Its flaky, buttery, pull-apart texture makes it irresistible. It's typically eaten with a simple grated tomato dip and slow-cooked eggs that are often cooked right on top of the bread in the same pan.

INGREDIENTS

- ½ cup water
- 4½ cups all-purpose flour
- 1¾ tsp dry yeast
- ⅓ cup granulated sugar
- 2 tsp salt

- 2 large eggs + 3 egg yolks
- ¼ cup olive oil
- 1 cup + 1 Tbsp unsalted butter (17 Tbsp), at room temperature

To serve:

• zhug (see page 12)   • huevos haminados (see page 20)

DIRECTIONS

1. Place the water, flour, yeast, sugar, salt, eggs and egg yolks in the bowl of a stand mixer fitted with the dough hook. Mix on a low speed for about 1 minute, until dough forms.

2. Increase the speed to medium-low and knead for 5-7 minutes until it forms a smooth, soft dough. Add the olive oil and knead until it's fully incorporated into the dough.

3. Shape the dough into a ball and place in a lightly greased bowl. Cover with a towel or a loose plastic wrap and let rise for 30 minutes at room temperature.

4. Punch down the dough, cover and let rise for another 30 minutes.

5. Grease an 8 inch cake pan (you can also use a springform pan or special tall kubaneh pan) generously with butter.

6. Divide the dough into 8 equal pieces, roll into balls and place on a greased plate. Brush the dough balls with butter and cover loosely with plastic wrap. Let rest for 10 minutes.

7. Grease your hands and the work surface with a spoonful of butter. Using your hands, press, flatten and stretch a dough ball into a large square as thin as you possibly can, without tearing it.

8. Fold the left and right sides of the dough in towards the center, creating a letter fold. Roll the dough all the way up from a short side to create a swirled cylinder. Repeat this with the remaining dough balls.

9. Using a sharp knife, cut each cylinder in half across the middle so it forms two tall swirls (they will look a little like taller cinnamon rolls). Place each piece in a single layer in the kubaneh pan, cut side facing up. Continue until the pan is full and you've used all the dough.

10. Brush some butter on top of the unbaked kubaneh, cover and let rise at room temperature for 1 hour.

11. Preheat the oven to 220°F. Cover the kubaneh with aluminum foil, making sure to leave the top loose, since the dough will continue to rise while baking.

12. Bake for 8-10 hours. Every 2 hours or so, brush the kubaneh with 1-2 tablespoons of butter.

13. Release the kubaneh from the pan and place on a cooling rack.

14. Serve with zhug (see page 12) and huevos haminados if desired (see page 20).

the
nosher

70/FACES
MEDIA

Made in the USA
Las Vegas, NV
21 June 2023

73714584R00036